WONDERFUL WORDS

Compiled by
Tammy Griffith

First published 2008

ISBN: 978-1-906381-04-2

Published by Autumn House Limited, Grantham, Lincolnshire
Printed in Thailand

Where possible the sources for quotes used have been given. Our
apologies for those sources left unacknowledged. If you wish to
notify us of the sources for quotes left anonymous, we will include
them in future publications.

All Bible texts are taken from the *Good News Bible* unless
otherwise stated.

Other versions used:
NKJV: *New King James Version*
NIV: *New International Version*
MGE: *The Message Bible*
ESV: *English Standard Version*
CEV: *Contemporary English Version*
NIRV: *New International Reader's Version*
NLT: *New Living Translation*

* Excerpts with this sign are taken from *'The Word 4u 2day'*.
Free issues of the daily devotional are available for the
UK & Republic of Ireland. Address: United Christian Broadcasters,
Freepost ST 1135, Stoke-on-Trent, ST4 8BR

It has always been my ambition to publish an inspirational book to encourage those going through personal trials.

In 1992, at the age of three, I was diagnosed with a brain tumour, which was successfully removed by surgery. However, I was left with several disabilities. With much help and support, I was able to work through these and accomplish many things: things which some thought were beyond my capabilities.

In 2000, my original symptoms reappeared. An MRI scan revealed that there was a re-growth of the brain tumour and its position ruled out further surgery. I underwent a full course of radiotherapy. This treatment was unsuccessful as the tumour kept on growing and entered my spinal cord. A full year's course of chemotherapy was prescribed. However, this treatment had to be aborted as my condition dramatically worsened. I was discharged from hospital on a programme of palliative care.

Through much prayer and with God's leading, I was introduced to alternative therapies in the form of homeopathy and acupuncture treatment. I had an immediate positive response to these. The medics describe me as a medical miracle!

During this difficult time, I was greatly encouraged by reading inspirational publications. Over the years, I have collected many of these encouraging thoughts, verses and Bible texts, which have helped to encourage me and strengthen my faith.

I am now eighteen, and about to start university – something which a few years ago seemed impossible.

May you be encouraged, inspired, and humoured by the words you read. May you be challenged to see life more positively. Most of all, I pray that the words within will remind you that 'God is Love'. He is interested in every aspect of your life. God hears even the smallest voice; he hears us whether we cry out to him in anger and frustration, or whisper in defeated desperation. I share this book with you, in the hope that the words within will bring you the comfort and assurance that they have brought me.

Tammy Griffith

CONTENTS

Wonderful words of . . .

PRECIOUS

Wisdom

'Nothing will stand in your way if you walk wisely.'

Proverbs 4:12

Life is not measured by the number of breaths we take, but by the number of moments that take our breath away.

Happiness is not about getting what you want, it's about enjoying what you have!*

The secret of living?

'Do what you can,
with what you have,
where you are.'
Theodore Roosevelt

'We make a living by
what we get. We make
a life by what we give.'
Winston Churchill

Our past can determine only our experiences, but not who we are.

*'As in a game of cards,
so in the game of life we must
play with what is dealt out to us;
and the glory consists not so much
in winning as in playing a poor
hand well.'*
Josh Billing

'Life belongs to the living, and he who lives must be prepared for changes.'
Johann Wolfgang von Goethe

Anybody can grow older. That doesn't take any talent or ability. The idea is to grow up, by always finding opportunity in change.

Use the talents you possess. The woods would be silent if the only birds that sang were the ones who sang best.

If you try to be good at everything, you'll end up good at nothing. God gave you specific gifts. Find them and use them.*

12

How you live is determined not so much by what life brings to you . . . as by the attitude you bring to life.

Whether you think you can, or you think you can't, you're right. Part of doing something difficult is believing that you can actually do it.

It takes commitment to change and an even deeper commitment to grow.

'Try not to become a man of success, rather a man of value.'
Albert Einstein

'The best use of life is to spend it for something that outlasts it.'
William Jaines

*'A journey of a thousand miles
must begin with a single step.'*
Chinese proverb

*'He who is outside the door
has already a hard part of his
journey behind him.'*
Dutch proverb

*'Even if you are on the right
track you'll get run over if you
just sit there.'*
Will Rogers

Luck is what happens when preparation meets opportunity. Like a bunch of keys, we've got to find the one that opens our particular door.

Only when you push yourself can you truly know what you can achieve.

When one door closes, another opens; but often we look so long at the closed door, that we do not see the other one which has opened for us.

Don't cry because it's over, smile because it happened.

Uttering a word is like breaking an egg – you can't put the pieces back together again.

Words slip easily from the tongue. Think well before you let them go.

Words are like medicine; they should be measured with care, for an overdose may hurt.

*'Think all you speak
but speak not all you think.'*
Patrick Delany

**Before you speak . . . listen.
And before you quit . . . try.**

*'Be careful how you think;
your life is shaped by your
thoughts.'*
Proverbs 4:23

There are two things over which you have complete dominion - your mind and your mouth.

God created us with one mouth and two ears; to tell us that we should spend twice as much time listening as we do talking.

What we do not overcome will overcome us, and work out our destruction.

Never underestimate the power of your actions; with one small gesture you can change a person's life, for the better, or for the worse.

'I expect to pass through this world but once; any good thing therefore that I can do, or any kindness that I can show to any fellow creature, let me do it now; let me not defer or neglect it, for I shall not pass this way again.'
Stephan Grellet

What we do in life
echoes into eternity.

'In any moment of decision
the best thing you can do
is the right thing, the next
best thing is the wrong
thing, and the worst
thing you can do is
nothing.'
Theodore Roosevelt

**People don't care
what you know,
until they know that
you care.**

People will forget what you
said, people will forget what
you did, but people will
never forget how you made
them feel.

Kindness is the oil that takes the friction out of life.

'You cannot do a kindness too soon because you never know how soon it will be too late.'
Ralph Waldo Emerson

'One of the most difficult things to give away is kindness – it is usually returned.'

C. Flint

'Kindness is a language that the deaf can hear and the blind can see.'
Mark Twain

WISE
Encouragement

*'Encouragement is
the oxygen of the soul.'*
John C. Maxwell

'When we long for
life without difficulties,
remind us that oaks grow
strong in contrary winds
and diamonds are made
under pressure.'
Peter Marshall

'Faith draws the poison from every grief, takes the sting from every loss, and quenches the fire of every pain; and only faith can do it.'*
Sidney Holland

Life's challenges are the soil in which faith grows.

When things get tough, always remember . . . faith doesn't get you *around* trouble it gets you *through* it!

Faith is what's left when there's nothing else to hang on to.

'Unbelief puts our circumstances between us and God. But faith puts God between us and our circumstances.'*
F. B. Meyer

'Great faith is a product of great fights.

Great testimonies are the outcome of great tests.

Great triumphs can only come after great trials.'

Smith Wigglesworth

Beyond the midnight there is morning.

'I will turn the darkness before them into light.'
Isaiah 42:16, ESV

God will guide us through the night, for we walk by faith and not by sight.

'Every sunrise is like a new page, a chance to receive each day in all its glory.'
Oprah Winfrey

'It is never too late – in fiction or in life – to revise.'
Nancy Thayer

It is important we remember that even though we might not think highly of ourselves, we are all gems in God's eyes.

The worth of our lives comes not in what we do or who we know, but who we are.

Life is:

A mystery, unfold it,
A journey, walk it,
Painful, endure it,
Beautiful, see it,
A joke, laugh at it,
Wonderful, enjoy it,
A candle, light it,
Precious, don't waste it,
A gift, open it,
Unlimited, go for it,
Light, shine in it.

*'Every life
is its own excuse for being.'*
Elbert Hubbard

**Are you feeling inferior?
God says you are his child.**

**Do you feel that your life is
worthless?**

**Jesus was prepared to do anything
for you – even to die for you.**

**You are special.
          Don't ever forget it.**

'Life is downright unfair.
And God knows it's
downright unfair from
personal experience.
God in Christ shared the
common lot of life with us
– with all its evils – but
has gained the victory
for himself and for us
if we trust him.'

Islwyn Rees

Looking to Jesus, my spirit is blest,
The world is in turmoil; in him
    I have rest;
The sea of my life around me
    may roar,
When I look to Jesus, I hear it no
    more.

"'In this world you will have trouble. But take heart! I have overcome the world.'"

John 16:33, NIV

GREAT
Love

'First learn to love yourself,
then you can love me.'
Bernard of Clairvaux

The best use of life is love.

The best expression of love
is time.

The best time for love is now.

**Love is the silken
cord that binds
hearts together.**

The only thing capable of turning an enemy into a friend is love.

Hate cannot drive out hate, only love can do it.

*'No matter what I say,
what I believe, and what
I do, I'm bankrupt without
love.'*
1 Corinthians 13:3, MGE

Life – love = nothing

Jesus gave up everything so you could have everything. He died so you could live forever.

Never again should you wonder what you have to be thankful for.

'What is love?
It is not that we loved God.
It is that he loved us and
sent his Son to give his life
to pay for our sins.

'Dear friends, since God
loved us that much, we
should also love one
another.'
1 John 4:10, 11, NIRV

God *(the greatest giver)*
so loved *(the greatest motive)*
the world *(the greatest need)*
that he gave *(the greatest act)*
his only begotten Son *(the greatest gift)*
that whoever *(the greatest invitation)*
believes in him *(the greatest opportunity)*
should not perish *(the greatest deliverance)*
but have everlasting life *(the greatest joy)*.
John 3:16, NKJV

GLORIOUS

Wisdom

'Getting wisdom is the most important thing you can do.'

Proverbs 4:7

After observing Mother Teresa's work
among the poor in Calcutta,
a reporter commented to her that
what she was doing was just
'a drop in the ocean.'

'Ah yes,' she replied,
'but the ocean is made up of drops.'

**Determined individuals
can make an enormous
difference to this world.**

Deal with yourself as an individual worthy of respect, and make everyone else deal with you the same way.

'Do not fear therefore; you are of more value than many sparrows.'
Matthew 10:31, NKJV

If you think you are too small to make a difference, try sleeping with a mosquito.

'You must be the change you wish to see in the world.'
Gandhi

'There's only one corner of the universe you can be certain of improving and that's your own self.'
Aldous Huxley

You can't change who you are, but you can change where you are going.

'Could we change our attitude, we should not only see life differently, but life itself would come to be different.'
Katherine Mansfield

'To know what is right and not to do it is cowardice.'
Confucius

'All that is needed for evil to triumph is for good men to do nothing.'
Edmund Burke

'If we do not maintain justice, justice will not maintain us.'
Francis Bacon

Justice delayed is justice denied, and the only things you regret in life are the things you never did.

Into each life some rain
must fall . . . but after the
rain new strength you'll gain.

**A calm sea never
made a good sailor.**

*'Our problems are the tools God
uses to polish us, not demolish us.'*
Mel Tari

*'There is no failure
except in no longer trying.'*
Elbert Hubbard

It is often through failure that success comes!

You are not defeated if you fall.
You are defeated if you don't get
back up.*

When things don't work out,
call them 'experiments',
not failures.

'Most people achieved their
greatest success one step beyond
what looked like their greatest
failure.'
Brian Tracy

Failure is not failure unless you learn nothing from it.

'Never let the fear of striking out get in your way.'
Babe Ruth

'Our greatest glory is not in never falling, but in rising every time we fall.'
Confucius

What is conceived in the mind, if believed, can be achieved.

'The key to realising a dream is not to focus on success but significance – and then even the small steps and little victories along your path will take on greater meaning.'
Oprah Winfrey

'The path to our destination is not always a straight one. We go down the wrong road, we get lost, we turn back. Maybe it doesn't matter which road we embark on. Maybe what matters is that we embark.'
Barbara Hill

'Arriving at one goal
is the starting point
to another.'

John Dewey

You can't build a reputation on what you are *going* to do.

If you wait for perfect conditions, you will never get anything done.

'God gives opportunities; success depends upon the use made of them.'
Ellen G. White

Waiting for an opportunity to do that thing you've always wanted – don't wait, make it happen. Noah didn't wait for his ship to come in, he built one.*

'The challenge is in the moment, the time is always now.'
James Baldwin

'You can't just sit there and wait for people to give you that golden dream, you've got to get out there and make it happen for yourself.'
Diana Ross

'GO FOR IT NOW! The future is promised to no one.'
Wayne Dyer

Being happy does not mean everything is perfect.

It means you have decided to see beyond the imperfections.

Success isn't instant.
Every great thing
has been built
exactly the same
way: bit by bit, step
by step, little by little.

'It matters not what you are thought to be, but what you are.'
Publius Syrius

We should spend less time trying to *look* good, and a lot more time actually *doing* good.

'It is not a calamity to die with dreams left unfulfilled, but it is a calamity not to dream.'
Benjamin Mays

The poorest man is not
the one without
a nickel, but the
one without a dream.

Humility is not thinking
less of yourself.
It is thinking of yourself less.

Pride is like sugar.
Too much is hard to swallow,
but stir in just a little
and you'll find
it sweetens everything!

'Beauty unaccompanied by virtue is a flower without perfume.'
French proverb

'Ask for help.
No one can whistle a symphony.
It takes a whole orchestra to play it.
Even the weak become strong
when they are united.'
Johann Friedrich von Schiller

LOVELY

Promise

'Promise a lot, and give even more.'
Anthony J. D'Angelo

Never promise more than you can perform.

'Underpromise, overdeliver.'
Tom Peters

'Promises are like crying babies in a theatre, they should be carried out at once.'

Norman Vincent Peale

There is an island
of opportunity in
the middle of every
difficulty.

**God's delays are
not God's denials.**

God gives us
what we need to know,
when we need to know it.

'If you look
at the world,
you'll be distressed.

If you look within,
you'll be depressed.

But if you look to Christ
you'll be at rest!'
Corrie ten Boom

'There is a friend who sticks closer than a brother.'

Proverbs 18:24, NKJV

Get to know him. His name is Jesus.

Come with your whole heart to Jesus, and you may claim his blessings.

'Delight yourself in the Lord and he will give you the desires of your heart.'
Psalm 37:4, NIV

When you get serious about finding me, and want it more than anything else, I'll make sure you won't be disappointed.

'The Lord has promised that he will not leave us or desert us.'
Hebrews 13:5, CEV

'Do not start worrying:
"Where will my food come from?
or my drink?
or my clothes? . . .
Your Father in heaven knows
that you need all these things."'
Matthew 6:31, 32

God knows your thoughts before you
think them; he knows when you wake
and when you lie down. When you
were growing inside your mother,
God was forming your body
and your emotions.

Whether you feel elated or depressed,
God will be with you, guiding you,
and holding your hand.
Summary of Psalm 139

*'Trust in the Lord with all your
heart. Never rely on what you
think you know. Remember the
Lord in everything you do, and
he will show you the right way.'*
Proverbs 3:5, 6

God's promises know no haste, and no delay for . . . God is never in a hurry, but he is always on time.

'God is our refuge and strength, an
ever-present help in trouble. Therefore
we will not fear, though the earth give
way and the mountains fall into the
heart of the sea . . . "Be still, and know
that I am God."'
Psalm 46:1, 2, 10, NIV

'The will of God will never lead you where the grace of God cannot keep you.'

John Henry Jowett

This means that the Lord won't demand something of you which he doesn't intend to help you implement.

'. . . with God all things are possible.'
Matthew 19:26, NKJV

Because . . . God doesn't just tell you what to do, he gives you the power to do it. *

'Be strong and courageous.
Do not be terrified;
do not be discouraged,
for the Lord your God will be
with you wherever you go.'
Joshua 1:9, NIV

"'These things I have spoken to you, that my joy might remain in you, and that your joy might be full.'"

John 15:11, NKJV

*"'My peace I give you;
not as the world gives
do I give to you.
Let not your heart be troubled,
neither let it be afraid.'"*

John 14:27, NKJV

When you make the biggest mistake ever, good can still come from it.

"'Though your sins are like scarlet,
They shall be as white as snow;
Though they are red like crimson,
They shall be as wool.'"
Isaiah 1:18, NKJV

'While we sinners are swimming against the tide, God is always on shore ready to throw us a lifeline.'
Dave Walkerton

'"Listen! I am standing and knocking at your door. If you hear my voice and open the door, I will come in and we will eat together."'
Revelation 3:20, CEV

Jesus will always respond when we reach out to him.

"'Come to me, all of you who are tired from carrying heavy loads, and I will give you rest.'"
Matthew 11:28

'Commit everything you do to the Lord. Trust him, and he will help you.'

Psalm 37:5, NLT

God promises
a safe landing,
not a calm passage.
If God brings you to it,
he will bring you
through it.

'If God is for us,
who can be against us?'
Romans 8:31

Nothing under God's control can ever be out of control. Mastered by him, you can handle anything.

*'Draw near to God and
he will draw near to you.'*
James 4:8, NKJV

*'You will seek me and find
me, when you search for
me with all your heart.'*
Jeremiah 29:13, NKJV

You are not, and never will be alone.

Jesus is beside you. He will walk with you through the shadows of life.

Just accept his outstretched hand.

'Do not fear, for I am with you; do not be dismayed, for I am your God. I will strengthen you and help you; I will uphold you with my righteous right hand.'
Isaiah 41:10, NIV

SPLENDID

Wisdom

'Hold on to your
wisdom . . .'
Proverbs 3:21

'Never try to make anyone
like yourself – you know,
and God knows, that one
of you is enough.'
Ralph Waldo Emerson

People who never change their mind are either perfect or (stupidly) stubborn.

Grudges are like babies –
the more you nurse them,
the bigger they grow.

*'There is no such thing
in anyone's life as an
unimportant day.'*
Alexander Woolcott

*'Remember, no one can make
you feel inferior without
your consent.'*
Eleanor Roosevelt

When you think the world
has turned its back on you,
take a look: you most likely turned
your back on the world.

All that time spent worrying
about what might happen,
means you miss out
on what is happening.

**Worry is the darkroom
in which negatives can develop.**

Worry is interest
paid on trouble
before it comes due.

*'For every minute you
are angry you lose sixty
seconds of happiness.'*
Ralph Waldo Emerson

**Always remember the compliments.
Forget the rude remarks.**

He who angers
you controls you.

The things that matter most
should never be at the mercy
of things that matter least.*

**If we don't live by priorities,
we will live by pressures.**

*'By failing to prepare,
you are preparing to fail.'*
Benjamin Franklin

Hard work is just an accumulation of the easy things you didn't do when you should have.*

Commitment is having the guts to follow through on your decisions.

'God helps those who help themselves.'
Benjamin Franklin

Another person's secret is like another person's money: you are never as careful with it as you are with your own.

The greatest of faults is to think you have none.

Money is like manure:
if you let it pile up it
stinks, if you spread it
around, it helps things
grow!*

**Your greatest
strength is to know
your weakness.**

Diplomacy gets you out of what tact would never have allowed you to get into in the first place.

God gave us memories so that we might have roses in December.

*'The more we count
the blessings we have,
the less we crave
the luxuries we haven't.'*
William A. Ward

Blessed is he who
can laugh at himself.
He has endless
amusement.

'Tell me – I forget
Show me – I remember
Involve me – I understand.'
Chinese proverb

**To teach is to
learn twice.**

'False friendship, like ivy, decays and ruins the walls it embraces.'
Richard Burton

Better to cry with another than to smile alone.

Good friends are like
stars . . . you don't always
see them but you know they
are always there.

The light of friendship is like
phosphorous – seen plainly when
all around is dark.

**Friendship improves happiness
and abates misery, by doubling
our joy and dividing our grief.**

Friends are those people
who ask how we are, and
then wait to hear the answer.

**A true friend is someone
who reaches for your hand
and touches your heart.**

A friend is someone who
believes in you, even when
you've ceased to believe in
yourself.

Words From On High

God doesn't call the qualified;
he qualifies the called.

Suffering from truth decay?
Brush up on your Bible.

When God is all we have,
we realise God is all we need.

Never doubt in the dark what God told you in the light.

Nothing else ruins the truth like stretching it.

Without God your jigsaw will always be missing a peace.

'Pray as if everything depended on God, and work as if everything depended on man.'
Francis Spellman

'God never made a promise that was too good to be true.'
Dwight L. Moody

Do not pray for an easy life, pray for the strength to endure a difficult one.

"'And surely I am with you always, to the very end of the age.'"
Matthew 28:20, NIV

EXTRAORDINARY

Love

Only time is capable of understanding how great love is.

'Life is a flower of which love is the honey.'
Victor Hugo

Life without love is a garden without flowers.

'Love me when I least deserve it, because that's when I really need it.'
Swedish proverb

'Love cures people – both the ones who give it and the ones who receive it.'
Carl Menninger

**God's love is unconditional.
Be sure that yours is too!**

'Love doesn't make the world go round. Love is what makes the ride worthwhile.'
Franklin P. Jones

Forgiveness is not just our greatest need, it is also God's highest achievement.

'God, who needs nothing, loves into existence wholly superfluous creatures in order that he may love and perfect them.'
C. S. Lewis

We walk with God only because he has gone to unimaginable lengths to enable us to do so.

Jesus loves me.
Not because I'm worthy of
his love. His love makes me worthy.*

When you are sleeping,
God gazes at you with love,
because you were his idea.
He loves you as if you were the only
person on Earth.

**God loves you!
He always has . . .
He always will.**

The greatest expression of sacrifice is the sacrifice of God's Son for you.

'God shows his love for us in that while we were still sinners, Christ died for us.'
Romans 5:8, ESV

If you want to know
how much you
matter to God, look
at Christ with his
arms outstretched
on the cross, saying,
'I love you this much!
I'd rather die than live
without you.'

"'You are worried and troubled over so many things, but just one is needed.'"
Luke 10:41, 42

Are you searching for truth?
Something which you can
wholeheartedly trust?
Do you want that inner
peace which so many seek,
but fail to find?

There is someone who
can take away every hurt,
every pain, all feelings of
resentment and frustration.

**There is only One that
you need – Jesus Christ.**

Unlike the quick fixes to life that are continually thrown at us, he offers you hope and eternal peace.

Why don't you say yes to his call today?